‖‖‖ ‖‖‖‖‖‖ ‖ ‖ ‖ ‖‖‖‖‖‖‖‖‖‖ ‖‖ ‖ ‖‖

W9-CEH-230

PILGRIM WOOD PUBLIC SCHOOL
1551 PILGRIM'S WAY
OAKVILLE, ONT. L6M 2W7

PLEASE RETURN TO
MISS MCCLOY

HOUSES AND HOMES

Alistair Hamilton-Maclaren

Illustrations by Jenny Hughes

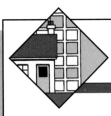

Exploring Technology

Communications
Flight
Houses and Homes
Land Transport
Machines
Structures
Textiles
Water Transport

Cover: Many inner-city industrial areas have been developed to provide attractive housing.

Series Editors: Sue Hadden and
William Wharfe
Book Editor: Joan Walters
Designer: Malcolm Walker, Kudos Designs

First published in 1991 by
Wayland (Publishers) Ltd
61 Western Road, Hove
East Sussex BN3 1JD, England

© Copyright 1991 Wayland (Publishers) Ltd

**British Library Cataloguing in
Publication Data**
Hamilton-Maclaren, Alistair
   Houses and homes. – (Exploring technology)
   I. Title   II. Series
   728.09

ISBN 0–7502–0211–4

Phototypeset by Kalligraphic Design Ltd,
Horley, Surrey
Printed in Italy by G. Canale & C.S.p.A.,
Turin
Bound in France by A.G.M.

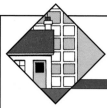

Contents

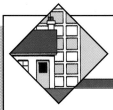

Introduction

Before people could build their own shelters they lived in caves. We know this because the walls of some caves are covered with drawings of what life was like for these early people. Cave dwelling worked well while there was a plentiful supply of food near the cave.

In prehistoric times people lived as nomads. They hunted for their food by following herds of animals as they too moved about the countryside in search of food. These people made shelters, called bivouacs, from whatever they could find: branches, stones and greenery. They were made quickly and often only used for a few days. They provided shelter from rain, wind and sunshine.

Life was easier when people learned to tame animals. An ox could be used to drag heavy branches from the forest to build a framework. Animal skins could be used to cover the framework, making a cosy tent that could be moved from site to site. Nomadic people, like the Bedouin of Arabia, live in tents. Bedouin tents are made from strong fabric woven from goat or camel hair.

In hot climates the sides of a tent can be rolled up to let in cooling breezes.

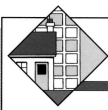

Build a bivouac

You will need
A junior hacksaw
A small garden spade
3 pieces of strong cord
3 wooden stakes
2 wooden poles 1.5 m long
A wooden pole 3 m long
Several leafy branches trimmed from a tree
Several small rocks
A hammer or wooden mallet

Before building a bivouac pick your site with care. You need an area of level ground close to a supply of foliage. Most important of all you need an adult's permission to use your chosen site and to trim branches from the trees.

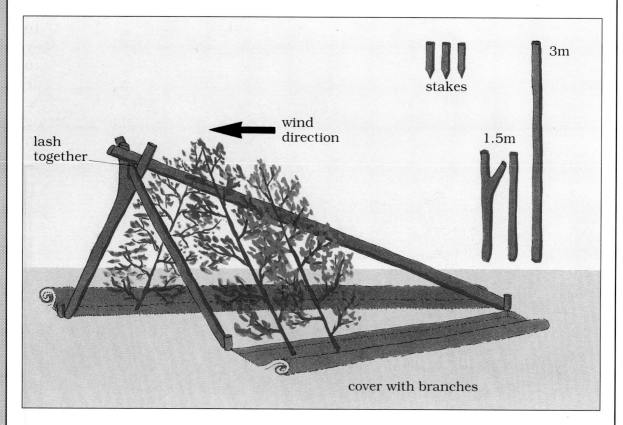

lash together

wind direction

stakes

3m

1.5m

cover with branches

1. Set up the poles and hammer in the anchor stakes. Lash together with strong cord as shown in the diagram.

2. Use the spade to cut and roll back the turf to form a gully down each side of the bivouac.

3. Cover the framework with enough leafy branches to form a thick roof that will keep out wind and rain.

4. Roll the turf back over the ends of the branches and weight down with a row of rocks.

Early buildings

Humans first worked out how to grow their own crops about 11,000 years ago. They no longer had to wander around searching for food. Because they knew that they would stay in the same place for a long time, they built themselves sturdy houses to live in. Transporting building materials was not easy, so houses were made from whatever materials were available locally.

Perhaps the most common building materials were mud and grass. The walls of a house were built from mud that was left to dry in the sun. The roof was made of a thick thatch of dried grass that overhung the walls keeping the whole house dry when it rained.

Mud is still used for building homes in hot dry climates. Today's mud houses are often round because the walls are less likely to

Mud bricks baked in the sun make good building units.

crack if the building has no corners. There are three common methods of constructing mud walls. The first is to make mud bricks and leave them to dry in the sun before assembling the house.

The second method is to make a timber mould the length and thickness of the wall. The mould is then filled with mud, straw and decorative stones. When the mud has hardened the mould can be moved up and refilled. In this way the wall can be built up layer by layer.

The third method is to build a timber framework. The wall space between the framework is then filled with woven branches. Finally, mud is plastered on to the woven frame to make smooth walls.

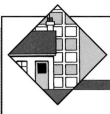

A model house

You will need
A round piece of cardboard 17 cm in diameter
35 wooden lollipop sticks
Cane and rafia for the walls and roof
Soft clay and a little water
A bradawl
A damp sponge
A pair of scissors
PVA glue
A forked stick 4 cm longer than lollipop sticks

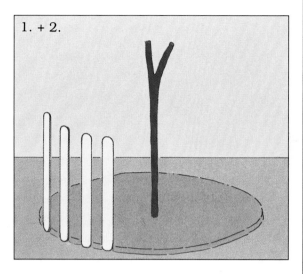

1. Using the bradawl, make a hole in the centre of the round cardboard base. Insert the forked stick into the hole and secure with glue.

2. Glue lollipop sticks at 1 cm intervals around the base. To make this easy, ensure that the sticks overlap the bottom of the base by 5 mm.

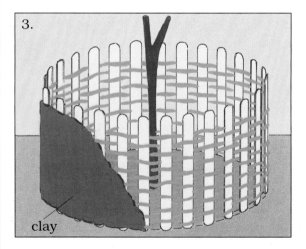

clay

3. Weave cane around the sticks to make the walls. Leave about 15 mm of wall sticks clear of cane. Work the clay with your fingers and a little water until it is soft and moist. Use the clay to plaster the outer walls of your house. Support the walls from the inside with your fingers and push the clay into the woven cane. Build up a layer of about 3 mm then smooth the walls with a damp sponge. Leave to dry.

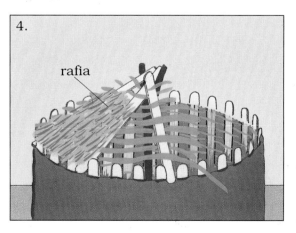

rafia

4. Now make a roof. Glue sticks from the central pole out to the walls. When the glue is dry weave some cane round the sticks to support the thatch. Use rafia to make a thatched roof.

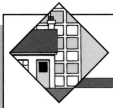

Building with timber

One of the most versatile building materials is timber. It is a renewable resource and can be easily cut, shaped and joined on site. Houses can be made entirely of timber but more often it is used with other materials. Look around your own home and make a list of the parts that are constructed of wood.

In some countries timber is a very expensive imported material. It is not uncommon to reuse large pieces, taken from demolished buildings, when new houses are built. Historically, another source of wood for building was timber that was salvaged from old ships or pieces washed up as driftwood on the sea-shore.

One disadvantage of using wood as a building material is that it rots. For this reason most timber is soaked with chemicals that stop fungus and insects from eating it. Timber that is exposed to severe weather is usually painted to keep it dry inside.

Some examples of wooden houses are the log cabins of the USA, Canada and Scandinavia. The cabins are built entirely from logs, notched at the corners to lock the walls together. The roofs are covered with timber shingles, or tiles, made from split logs.

Log cabins under construction in Finland where timber is plentiful.

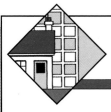

A model log cabin

You will need

About 30 small sticks
A piece of cardboard
    15 cm × 20 cm
Panel pins

Soft clay
PVA glue
A junior hacksaw

1. Following the diagrams, aim to build your model log cabin one layer at a time. Glue two sticks side by side, about a stick-length apart, on to the cardboard base. Glue more sticks on top of the first two but at right angles to them. Continue to build layers leaving gaps for a window and a doorway. Use small pieces of stick either side of the window and the doorway.

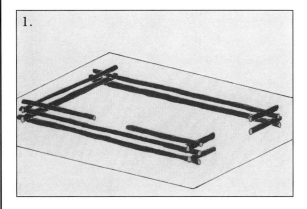

1.

2. As you build each layer, cut the sticks to size to make supports for a window and a doorway. Glue them in place as shown.

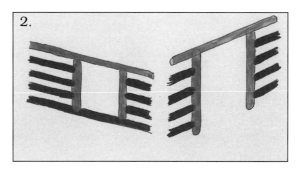

2.

3.

clay

3. Continue to build layers above the doorway in the shape of a pyramid. Repeat above the opposite wall. Fill in gaps with soft clay pushed right through and smoothed off on both sides.

4. Lay a stick on top of the pyramids to join them. Attach with panel pins. This will act as a support for the roof. Make the roof by gluing sticks, side by side, on either side of the support.

4.

Stone and brick buildings

A place of prayer built entirely of stone in the south west of Ireland.

For thousands of years people have used stones to build shelters. The stones can be laid to interlock without a binding mortar. Openings for doors and windows can be made with long stones called lintels. It is still possible to see dry-stone walls today. Many fields are surrounded by these walls to keep animals from straying.

As building skills improved, lintels were sometimes replaced by beautifully-constructed arches. Old buildings can sometimes be dated by the shape of these arches. Self-supporting arches were used to make bridges across rivers and valleys. Some of these stone bridges built hundreds of years ago are still used today.

The skills of quarrying and shaping stone enabled people to make more intricate buildings. Fine examples of the stone mason's art are churches and castles. The cellars in these buildings have stone ceilings. The stones arch over to form the roof and the floor of the next storey. In some places, bricks are a much more common building material than stone or timber. The strongest bricks are regular-shaped blocks of clay, which are left to dry and then fired in a very hot kiln (like an oven). The bricks are held together with mortar. Once the mortar has dried the brick wall, pillar or arch is very strong indeed. The most important rule of brick laying is to stagger the joints so that the bricks are interlocked (see picture). Different styles of doing this have developed in different countries.

A lot of modern buildings are constructed from large manufactured blocks made of concrete. These blocks are equivalent to several bricks and can be laid quickly but are less attractive than bricks. To improve their appearance the blocks are covered with a layer of render (cement and sand mixed together with water) before the building is painted.

A timber frame may be built to support a brick arch during construction. When the mortar has set, the wooden frame is removed.

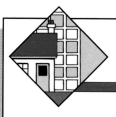

A bridge-building challenge

You will need
About 20 wooden blocks approximately
   9 cm × 3 cm × 1.5 cm
A small toy car

Using the wooden blocks with care, it is possible to build a bridge, or an archway.

1. Following the diagram, build your bridge by laying each block so that it overlaps the lower one by not more than a third of its length. Build up the bridge evenly from either side. Weight the backs of the blocks with more blocks.

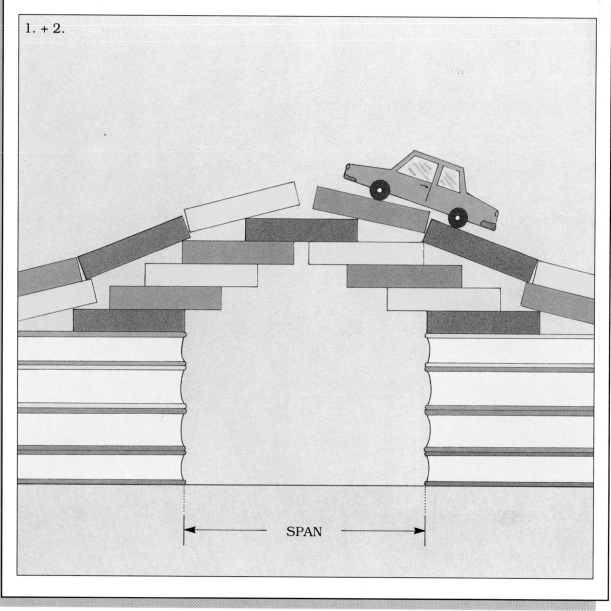

1. + 2.

SPAN

2. When the bridge is completed try to push the toy car over the top. Will it fit under the bridge?

3. Try to think of other ways to make bridges and arches with wooden blocks.

Many different sizes of stones have been used to build this bridge.

Working houses

Most people used to work where they lived so houses were built to provide work areas as well as living accommodation. For example, in areas where bad weather, like heavy snow, could trap people in their houses for long periods, a farm was often one building. The animals and winter feed were kept under the same roof as the farmer and his family.

The village blacksmith seldom allowed the fire in the forge to go out. This meant that his house needed to be close by. Millers lived in the windmills so that corn could be ground when the wind blew, day or night. Shopkeepers, like bakers or clockmakers, usually had a work area in the shop where their products were manufactured.

Lighthouse keepers often had to survive for many weeks during bad weather before supplies could be sent to them. The lighthouse had to have plenty of storage space for the keeper's food and fuel for the lamp. Lighthouses are built of interlocking stones set right into solid rock. They have to resist perpetual buffeting from the sea. Today, most lighthouses work automatically without the need of a keeper. When lighthouses are lived in, the keepers are often supplied by helicopter.

The lighthouse at Cape Victoria, Australia.

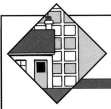

Make a model lighthouse

You will need
A piece of hardboard 35 cm × 35 cm
A piece of wire mesh 45 cm × 45 cm
Wallpaper paste and water
Finely shredded newspaper
PVA glue
Poster paints and paintbrush
An empty, clear plastic bottle
A small, round plastic container
A cardboard tube
An old plastic bowl
A wooden spoon

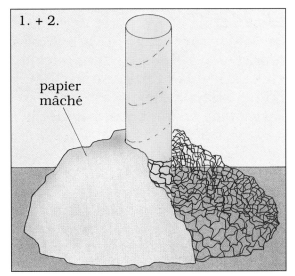

1. + 2.

papier
mâché

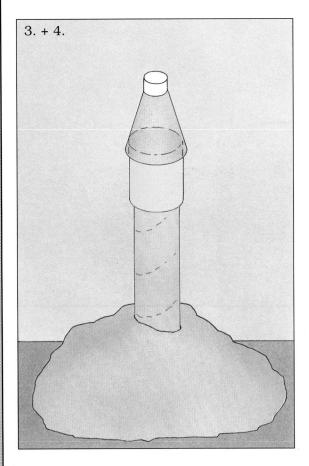

3. + 4.

1. Make up some papier mâché in the bowl by mixing shredded newspaper, wallpaper paste and water and stirring well until the paper is very soggy and the mixture is quite thick.

2. Crumple the wire mesh into a rocky shape and place it on to the baseboard. Put the cardboard tube on top of the mesh.
 Cover the whole structure with papier mâché and leave to dry.

3. When dry, glue the plastic container on top of the tube. Cut the bottom off the plastic bottle and glue it to the container (see diagram).

4. Use blue and white paint to make the sea around the edges of the baseboard. Use other colours to paint the rocks and the lighthouse.

5. Can you think of a way to put a light into the top of your lighthouse? See page 23.

15

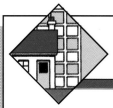

Building houses

Today, most people have to put forward plans to a council for approval before a new house can be built. There are also strict controls over how materials are used. These ensure that new houses are safe to live in and will not use up too much energy for heating and lighting.

When a building site is agreed upon it must be prepared. Valuable topsoil is scraped off and piled up to use again later. This may be done by hand but one person can complete the job quickly using a mechanical digger. Foundations are then prepared for the house to stand on. These may be trenches cut in the ground and filled with concrete. If the ground is soft then concrete poles, known as piles, are driven into the ground and the house is built on these. Essential services such as water, drainage and gas supply pipes and electricity cables are then installed to be connected later.

For houses and small apartment blocks the next step is to build the walls. For large tower blocks a steel skeleton built of girders is erected. The spaces between the girders are filled in with blocks or large panels.

When the ground floor is built, joists of timber or concrete span the walls to carry the upstairs floors. When the roof level is reached a timber framework is built to carry the roof covering. Roof timbers were traditionally built on site, but now prefabricated roof trusses are made to the customer's specifications and transported to the site by lorry. The timber framework is then quickly assembled in place ready for the roof covering.

Foundations to support a building may be dug deep into the ground and filled with reinforced concrete.

Timber-framed houses can be built quickly using factory-made parts.

One of the oldest roofing materials, thatch, is now rare. Kiln-baked clay tiles are a popular roof covering. However, in recent years concrete tiles have become more common. Concrete tiles can be coloured and textured to give just the right effect. Other materials used are slates, sheets of copper, aluminium or lead, and asphalt on flat roofs. When the outer shell of the house is complete the builders start to fit the interior.

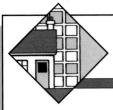

Building skills

When a house is being built it is important to ensure that the floors are level and the walls are perfectly upright. The taller the building the more critical this becomes. Builders use an instrument called a spirit level to check floors and walls. This consists of a block in which a sealed tube partially filled with liquid has been set so that an air bubble rests between two marks on the tube when the block is perfectly horizontal.

Make a plumb-line

A plumb-line can be used to find out if a wall is being built perfectly upright (see diagram). It can also be used to draw a vertical line on an inside wall so that wallpaper can be hung straight.

1. Tie a weight on to the end of a piece of string.

2. Use the drawing pin to fix the other end of the string to the wall.

3. Let the weight hang freely on the end of the string. When it stops swinging use the pencil to draw a line on the wall following the string. This line can be used as a guide to hang wallpaper so that it is straight.

You will need
2 syringe barrels
3 m clear plastic tube
A jug of water
A few drops of food colouring
A length of string 2 m long
A small, heavy weight
A pencil
A drawing pin

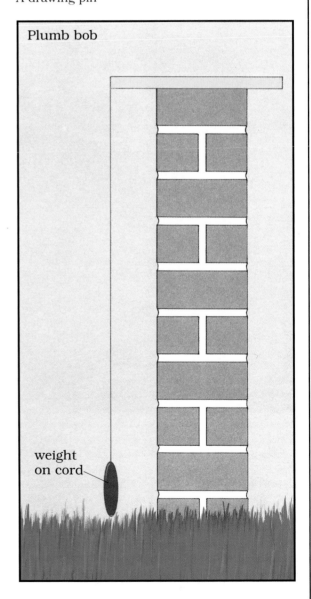

Plumb bob

weight on cord

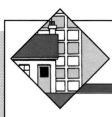

Build a water level

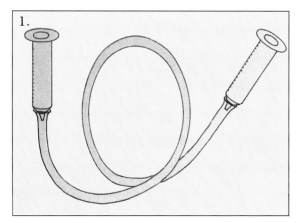

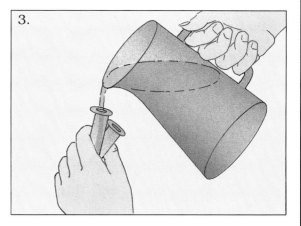

1. Connect a syringe barrel to each end of the plastic tube.

2. Mix a few drops of food colouring into the water.

3. Carefully pour the coloured water into one syringe only (this will prevent air bubbles forming) until the tube is full and both syringes are half filled.

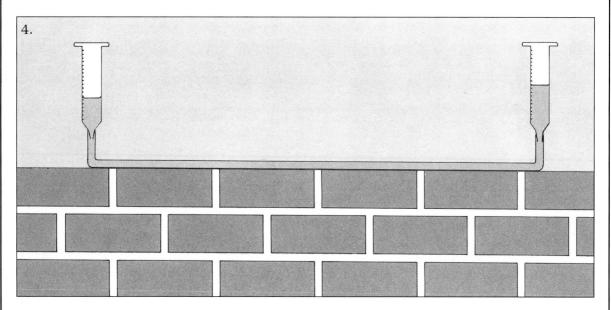

4. To check that a surface is level, lay the tube on it. When something is perfectly level, the water in both syringes will rest on the same mark on the syringe scale. Try this out on all kinds of surfaces: the kitchen table, or your garden wall for example.

Windows

Natural light has always been valued, especially before the times of gas and electric lamps. But windows let in draughts and so are often quite small. Glass was very expensive in the past and difficult to produce in large sheets until the nineteenth century. Before this time shutters were fitted over windows. They provided shade with ventilation in hot areas and protection against stormy weather in cold climates.

In some countries, like France, shutters are still popular and windows normally open inwards. The shutters can therefore be operated from inside the house and the windows can be open when the shutters are closed. In countries where shutters are seldom seen, windows tend to open outwards. This makes them difficult to clean from the inside.

Before glass became available in big sheets, window frames were constructed in two ways. The first way was to make the frame out of small square panes. The glass for these was produced by blowing a ball of glass then spinning the ball flat.

The other method of producing large windows was to fix small diamonds of glass together with lead strips. This method has been particularly effective in churches and entrance halls where the glass has been stained to produce patterns and pictures.

A lot of the heat in a house is lost through the windows. To reduce this, modern windows are produced with two or three layers of glass, separated by an insulating air gap. This is called double (two layers) or triple (three layers) glazing.

Restoring a stained glass window preserves a building's character.

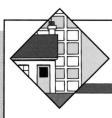

A stained glass window

You will need
Some scrap paper
A pencil
A white crayon or a piece of chalk
A large piece of black paper
Coloured cellophane paper
(Sweet wrappers can be used)
PVA glue
A craft knife (**Use with care**)
A cutting mat
(A thick layer of newspaper can be used)
Sticky tape

1. Sketch some designs for a stained glass window.

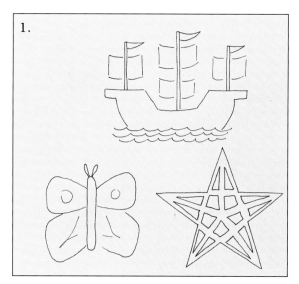

2. Draw or trace the outline of your favourite design on to the black paper.

3. Ask an adult to help you cut out your chosen design using the craft knife.

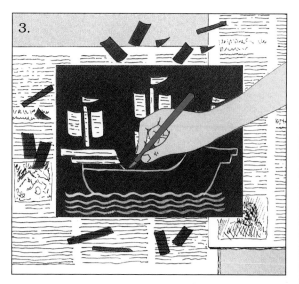

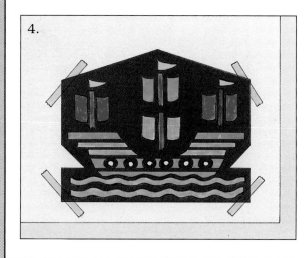

4. Glue coloured cellophane over the cut outs. Trim the outer shape of your picture and tape to a window with the cellophane against the glass.

Electricity

Modern homes could not be run without electricity. It is used for heating, lighting and cooking, and to run equipment like fridges and televisions. Cables, connected to a supply from the power company, enter the house and are fed through a meter. The meter records how much electricity is used in that house and a bill is sent by the power company to the residents of the house. Wires sunk into the walls of the house carry the electricity to sockets and light switches.

Mains electricity is very dangerous. Only a qualified electrician should make any alterations to a system. Most electric appliances need a plug which is fitted with a fuse. A fuse is a deliberate weak link in the electrical system which prevents an appliance (such as a kettle or an iron) drawing too much electricity. If a fuse burns out, the appliance that caused the problem should be properly checked before a new fuse of the correct rating is fitted.

An earth leakage circuit breaker can provide protection against a faulty appliance. It cuts off the electricity within a fraction of a second at the first sign of trouble.

Electricity provides light and warmth making life more comfortable for this family.

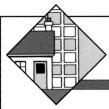

A two-way switch

You will need
A wooden baseboard 15 cm × 5 cm
2 × 1.5v batteries and a battery pack
1 × 3v bulb and bulb holder
6 drawing pins
2 paperclips
Insulating tape
Thin insulated wire

1. Tape the battery pack and the bulb holder to the base.

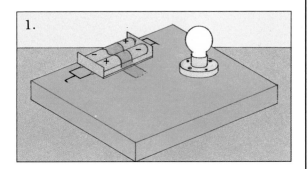

2. With the insulation stripped off the ends of the wires connect one wire from the batteries to the bulb holder and another wire from the batteries to a paperclip. Push a drawing pin through the paperclip to hold it on to the baseboard.

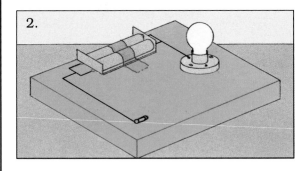

3. Connect a wire from the bulb holder to a second paperclip held to the board by a drawing pin.

4. Set the other four drawing pins so that contact can be made between them and the paperclips. Join these pins with wire as shown in the diagram.

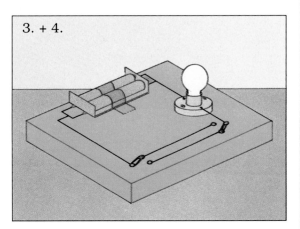

5. To operate the light move the paperclips to make contact between two drawing pins. The light can be switched on or off by moving either paperclip to the other pair of pins.

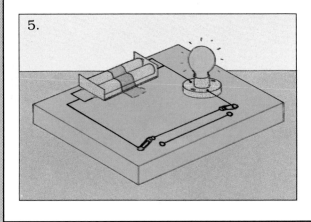

6. Where do you think two-way switches would be useful in your home?

Heating and cooling

Wood or coal fires were traditionally used for heating and cooking. Then stoves were developed to work as cookers and as boilers to operate hot water and central heating systems. Boilers can be made to operate on gas, oil, electricity or solid fuel.

Central heating is the best way to heat a home. The most common form of central heating pumps hot water to radiators around the house. A thermostat controls the temperature of the radiators and a time switch can be used to operate the system automatically.

A coal fire is warm and attractive.

Being too hot can be just as uncomfortable as being too cold. An air conditioner reduces the temperature in a house or room. Air is cooled when a fan blows it across a refrigeration unit situated inside the building. The heat removed from the air is released outside the house.

An important effect of lowering the temperature in a room is that it reduces humidity. Reduced humidity cuts down condensation and therefore the growth of moulds.

Heating and cooling systems use large amounts of energy. Energy is expensive and so it is important to use as little as possible. The easiest and simplest way to make our homes more efficient is to insulate them. This also cuts down on the air conditioning needs.

The best way to insulate a house is to build it in during construction using effective materials. Thick layers of padding in the roof spaces trap air and insulate very well. Draught-proofing doors and windows stops a lot of hot or cold air escaping. Double- or triple-glazed windows are even more effective.

Burning fossil fuels to make energy pollutes our environment. There are cleaner sources of energy such as the wind and the sun. Even in temperate climates a lot of heat can be collected with solar panels.

As technology advances solar panels can be linked to hot water systems. Heat is extracted from a source outside the house and released either into the hot water or the central heating system through a heat pump. Unfortunately the initial high costs of collecting solar energy has prevented many people from using this system.

As technology advances solar panels become more efficient.

Make a solar collector

You will need
1 rubber bung
An empty wooden fruit box
A long length of garden hose
Matt black emulsion paint and brush
A supply of pipe clips and screws
Insulation block to fit fruit box
Aluminium foil
Clear plastic sheeting and sticky tape
Cold water supply (garden tap)

1. Paint hose with black paint and leave to dry. (Dark colours absorb more heat than light colours.)

2. Stick reflective foil on to insulation block and fit into fruit box.

3. Use pipe clips to fix hose, in loops, on to insulation block.

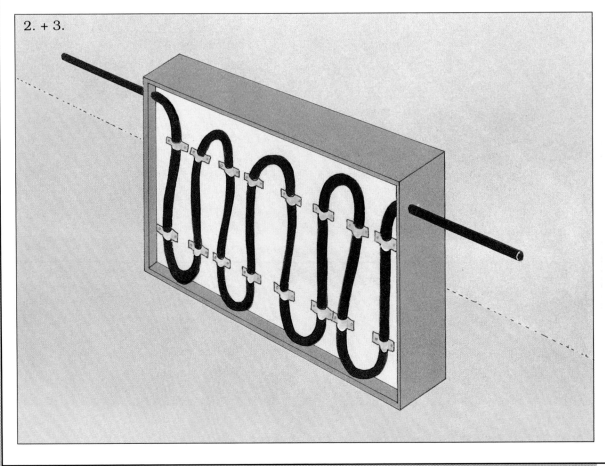

4. Cover the box with clear plastic. Connect one end of the hose to the cold tap. Fill the hose with water then disconnect. Close one end with a rubber bung. Support the other end so that the water does not run out.

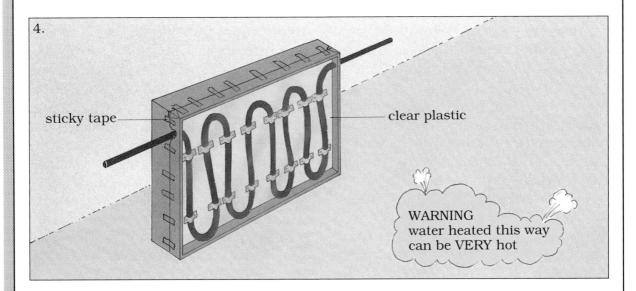

4.

sticky tape

clear plastic

WARNING
water heated this way
can be VERY hot

5. Leave your solar collector in a sunny position for a couple of hours. Even on a dull day the water in the hose should warm up.

Water warmed in this way is great for washing bikes and cars or for filling a paddling pool. Think of some other ways you could use it.

Water heated in a solar collector could be used to wash cars.

Water

Most people in the developed world take water for granted. We turn on the tap and water pours out. We use large quantities of water every day for washing machines, dishwashers, toilets and for personal hygiene. If we had to draw water from a well or pump and carry it home, we would use it much more carefully.

Tap water comes from water treatment plants. The water is processed and analysed to ensure it is as fresh and clean as possible. Waste water is also treated and recycled to be used again.

In our homes a cold-water storage tank holds a supply of water for immediate use. The quantity is maintained by a float valve that lets water flow into the tank as the level in it drops. The valve turns off the supply when the correct level is restored. Some of this water passes to a hot-water tank where it is heated by one of two methods. An element, like that found in an electric kettle, can heat the water until a thermostat switches it off. Alternatively, water can be passed through a tube inside the tank which is heated by a boiler. When the water in the tank reaches a certain temperature a thermostat shuts off the boiler.

Hot and cold running water makes washing an easy task.

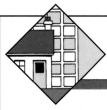

Make a water siphon

You will need
An empty plastic ice-cream tub
A bendy straw
A small wooden brick
PVA glue
Sticky tape
A jug of water
A craft knife (**Use with care.**)

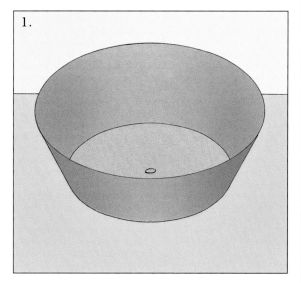

Every time you flush the toilet you are operating a siphon. To see how this works, make your own siphon by following these instructions.

1. Cut a hole in the bottom of the plastic tub just the right size for the straw to fit snugly.

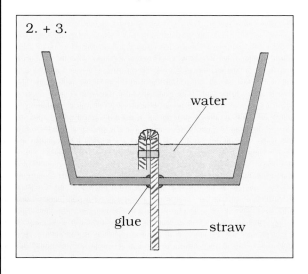

2. Bend the top end of the straw and fix into a U-shape with sticky tape. Slide the straw through the hole so that the short, bent end is just above the bottom of the tub. Glue in place to make a watertight seal.

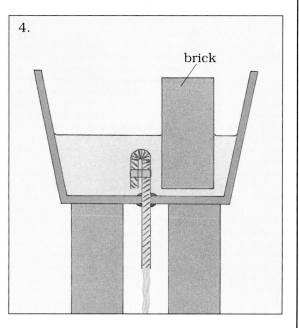

3. Fill the tub with water to just below the bend in the straw.

4. Support the tub over a basin and lower the brick into the water. Watch what happens. As the water level rises the siphon action is started and the tub begins to empty through the straw.

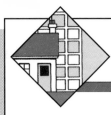

Furnishings

Homes are not just empty buildings. We use furnishings to make life more comfortable. All kinds of homes have carpets. Beautiful woven rugs are used in the tents of Bedouins and in Mongolian yurts. Many homes have wall-to-wall carpeting which is comfortable to walk on. It also reduces noise and insulates the floor.

Furniture differs from country to country depending on the climate. Beds are sometimes wooden platforms or blanket rolls on the ground. Dining tables are common in places where cooking is done inside. Where cooking is done outside and houses are used mainly for shelter, dining tables are very rare. Curtains give privacy and keep out draughts.

Kitchens in the developed world have changed a lot. We now have built-in storage units to hold pots and pans, crockery and preserved food. Cookers, refrigerators and other appliances are enclosed in the units to provide neat, clean work surfaces.

Draw up a list of the items in your own home that you would find it very difficult to live without. Discuss this list with a friend. Work out just how much is really essential!

A family sit down at the dining table for tea.

Furniture from scrap

You will need

Wooden pallets	An old plastic bowl	A hammer
Used bricks	A wooden spoon	A junior hacksaw
Corrugated cardboard	A piece of plastic sheeting	Glasspaper
Shredded newspaper	Wooden skewers	Paints and brushes
Wallpaper paste and water	Sticky tape	

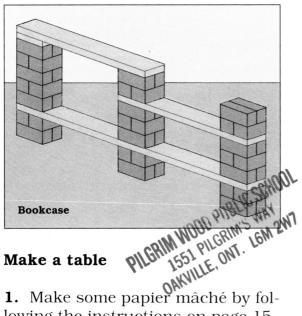

Bookcase

Make a table

1. Make some papier mâché by following the instructions on page 15.

2. Cover a flat surface with a sheet of plastic. Build up layers of papier mâché on the plastic. Leave to dry slightly before adding the next layer.

3. When dry and hard, peel off the plastic. You are left with a board which you can trim to shape with a junior hacksaw.

4. Roll up corrugated card and secure with tape to make four legs and four connecting rails. Cover each one with papier mâché and leave to dry.

Build a bookcase

1. Carefully break up the wooden pallets and select suitable pieces to use as shelves.

2. Rub the wood smooth with glass-paper.

3. Make sure your bricks are clean.

4. Assemble the bookcase by sandwiching the shelves between stacked bricks.

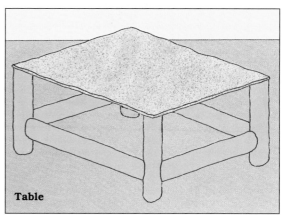

Table

5. Put your table together using wooden skewers as nails and papier mâché as glue.

6. When really hard and dry, smooth with glasspaper then decorate.

PILGRIM WOOD PUBLIC SCHOOL
1551 PILGRIM'S WAY
OAKVILLE, ONT. L6M 2W7

Labour-saving devices

This kitchen has many labour-saving devices.

Modern homes have many devices to save us work. Almost all of them need electricity in some way or another. Electric motors are used to drive all kinds of equipment from washing machines to carving knives, food mixers to vacuum cleaners.

We use refrigerators and freezers to keep food for long periods and save time spent shopping. Some garage doors can be opened by the car driver operating a control box from inside the car. The control box sends invisible, infra-red signals to a sensor on the motor that lifts the door.

In some blocks of flats the front door to the building can be controlled by the residents from their own flat. An intercom system outside the door is linked to each flat. Visitors use the intercom to call the flat. If the person in the flat wants to see the visitor, he or she presses a button to unlock the outside door. This system saves long trips up and down stairs and should keep out unwanted visitors.

The most common automatic system in homes controls the central heating, or air conditioning. A time switch can be set to turn the heating or hot water on and off. Additional sensors can control the systems if it suddenly turns very cold outside.

Home computers can be linked to large 'mainframe' computers by telephone. This means that people can work from home and do not waste time travelling to an office.

There are many other time-saving gadgets for the home. For example, at the press of a button you can open or close the curtains, change the television programme or operate the compact disc player.

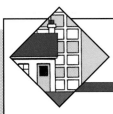

Make a bell

You will need
Several metres of nylon fishing line
A small bell on a spring (fishing bite indicator)
A length of plastic tube
Sticky tape
A pair of scissors
A rubber band
An empty cotton reel
Two screws and two nails
A wooden base
A small piece of plywood for pivot
A hammer
A bradawl or a drill

You can rig up a bell system between any two rooms at home or at school.

1. Following the diagrams, build the bell unit and test. It should be easy to pull and the bell should wobble and keep ringing.

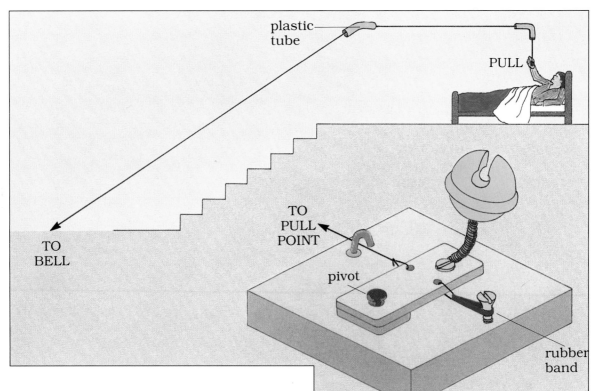

2. Decide which rooms you want to connect with a bell system and work out your route. The nylon cord should run in a series of straight lines where nobody will trip over it. Tape a length of plastic tube at every corner bent to the required change of direction.

3. Fix the bell unit in place. Thread the nylon line from the pivot, along your route, through the plastic tubes to the pull point. Tie the cotton reel to the line for a handle.

Tower blocks

Where ground space is scarce but there are a lot of people to house, one solution is to build tower blocks. Each block contains many individual apartments.

Building tower blocks requires special techniques. The foundations for the building are cut deep into the ground. Where the ground is soft, hundreds of long concrete posts, known as piles, are forced into the earth before the concrete base is laid. A framework of steel girders is then built up. The steel at the base of the building is the heaviest because it must support the building above it. As the framework gets higher, lighter girders are used.

The steel girders are cut and drilled before they arrive on the building site. They are lifted into position by tower cranes. The tower cranes are built up in the lift shafts of the building and 'jumped up' as the framework gets higher.

Modern blocks are constantly checked during construction by laser surveying instruments. Laser beams always travel in straight lines and are very useful in checking that a building is perfectly upright. Before the steel framework is finished, work begins on completing the lower floors. Scaffolding is used to ensure that the workers are safe while they build the walls.

Crane drivers move heavy materials all over a building site.

Tower blocks have to be designed so that each floor is fireproof and soundproof. In case of fire, pipes are built into the structure through which firefighters can pump water or foam from the street to the required floor. Lifts are needed to transport people up and down the floors. Fireproof stairways to each floor are also provided in case the lifts are not working. Services (water and gas pipes and electricity cables) have to be easily accessible for regular maintenance. The outside parts of a tower block (walls and windows) should be designed so that they do not need frequent maintenance or cleaning.

Drying laundry and disposing of rubbish can be a problem for people living in a tower block. Some blocks

The gardens surrounding these flats are shared by the occupants.

have special facilities for the disposal of soft household rubbish like food. Grinders in sinks chop it up before it is flushed down waste pipes. Other rubbish can be sent, via a chute, from each apartment to huge bins in the basement. Many blocks of flats have special rooms with extra ventilation where residents can dry their laundry.

The basement of a tower block can also provide off-street parking and dry access to the apartments above. Road access to car parks, community areas for meeting and playing all have to be considered when the building is being designed.

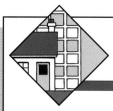

Recycling rubbish

You will need
Several large strong boxes
A pen and paper
Access to a photocopier
Adult supervision
An old pram or shopping basket on wheels

A large group of people living together in one building could co-operate in a rubbish recycling project. Before starting this project you must ask for permission and help from your parents. You must also live in or near a block of flats.

1. Write a notice to explain your recycling ideas. Ask residents if they will agree to help. You could design a tear-off slip at the end of the notice for people to return giving their permission.

```
                              Residents Association
                              Rosehill Apartments
                              Pinky Lane
                              Blue Town

Dear Resident
Rosehill Apartments Recycling Project
At our last meeting we decided to organize
a recycling project. We would like to
collect glass, aluminium cans, newspapers
and magazines.
If you would be willing to save these items
from your rubbish please return the tear-off
slip below.
We hope you will be able to support this
worthwhile project.
- - - - - - - - - - - - - - - - - - - - - - - - - - - - - - - -
PLEASE RETURN TO APARTMENT 34

Name ...........................
Apartment no ....................
I do/do not wish to support this project.
Any comments:
```

2. Visit your local supermarket/greengrocer and collect several strong cardboard boxes. These can be used as 'bins' for empty bottles, used paper, aluminium cans and any other 'rubbish' you would like to collect for recycling.

ALUMINIUM CANS

CLEAR GLASS

PAPER

COLOURED GLASS

3. Find out where your local collection points are located – e.g. bottle-banks, scrap metal merchants.

4. Set a day in the week for transporting collected rubbish to collection points.

Warning: Ask people to rinse bottles and cans so that rubbish does not get smelly and attract flies or rats.

These children are making their own recycled paper. Each sheet has to be hung out to dry.

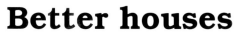# Better houses

Existing houses can be improved to make life more comfortable and save energy. New houses should include energy-efficient features.

Insulation built into a house saves energy. Cavity walls help to keep a house dry and if the inside wall is made of thick, aerated concrete blocks, heat loss will be kept to a minimum. Insulation of 300 mm in the roof space reduces the loss of rising heat. In some countries, like Sweden, windows are triple glazed to keep out the cold. Doors that fit well into their frames prevent draughts and a heat exchanger system to ventilate the building, more than recovers the operating costs. The materials used on the outside of the house should also be considered. Treating timber with preservative before use saves on painting.

Additional savings can be made inside the house. Modern central heating boilers require less space and are more efficient since they use much less fuel than early models. Modern washing machines and toilet systems use less water.

More use could be made of solar power to heat buildings. Community heating systems that make use of geothermal springs or surplus hot water from industry have been developed very successfully in some countries. We too can save energy by making a real effort to recycle as much of our waste as possible.

Putting new double-glazed windows into an old house makes it more energy-efficient. A lot of heat escapes from old, draughty windows.

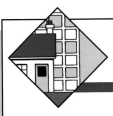

Testing insulation

You will need
3 cups – 1 paper, 1 plastic, 1 polystyrene
A measuring jug
A bucket of water
18 ice cubes
A wooden lollipop stick (for stirring)
Sticky tape
Old newspapers
A clock
A pen, a ruler and paper

1. Draw up a chart like the one below.

cup material	melting time	
	uninsulated	insulated
paper		
plastic		
styrofoam		

2. Put your cups on some newspaper. Measure out an equal quantity of water into each cup.

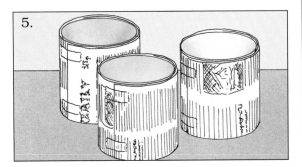

3. Make a note of the time on your chart then drop three identical ice cubes into each cup. Every five minutes give the ice four stirs with the lollipop stick.

melted

4. Make a note on your chart of how long it takes for the ice to melt in each cup. What conclusions can you draw from your results?

5. Repeat the experiment but this time insulate the cups by wrapping a cylinder of newspaper round each one.

Special houses

Very few houses are built to support people with special needs. Often only minor changes are needed to make life much easier. It is important to realize that many people who are not obviously physically handicapped may have special needs. For example, some people may wish to live alone and so do not need a big house. An artist who works at home needs a studio with lots of natural light. Working musicians may need to have their homes made sound-proof so as not to disturb neighbours.

Special equipment is available to give physically handicapped people a greater level of independence. Frames around toilets and baths make them easier and safer to use. Low level fittings, like public telephones, help people in wheelchairs. Simple activities, such as pulling a plug from its socket, are difficult for people with arthritis in their hands. Extra large plugs with handles can help but often the people who need them do not know that they exist.

Talk to some elderly or disabled people and make a list of activities that they find difficult. Organize these in order of priority and research what is available to help each particular problem. Try not to stop at the first possible solution but produce a chart of choices. The best place to start research is your local library. Look for voluntary associations that give specialized help.

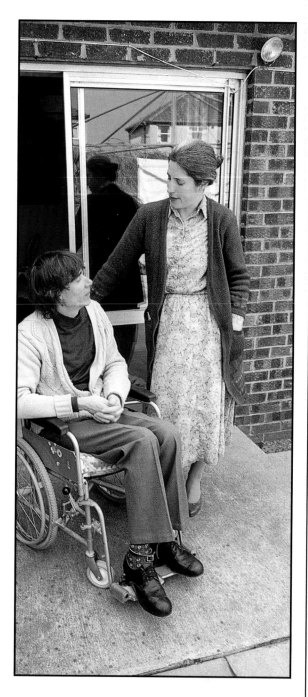

There are many ways to adapt a house for handicapped people.

40

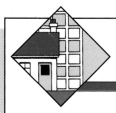

Project challenge

You will need
A pen and paper

'Special needs' does not always apply to a person confined to a wheelchair. Short people find it hard to reach high shelves. Old people often find it difficult to open jars and bottles. Do you know somebody with a disability – minor or major? Ask them if you can help in any way. Discuss their problems with them and make a list of helpful ideas. Research your ideas and try to solve your friend's difficulties.

If you do not know anybody with a problem that you could solve, here are some ideas to think about:

1. How could a partially-sighted or blind person match the right socks together?

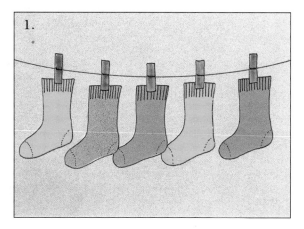

2. How could a deaf person know that the fire bell is ringing?

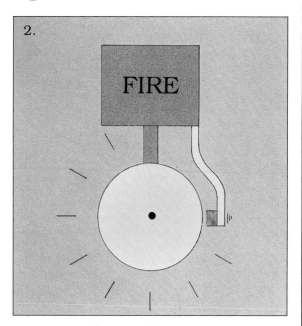

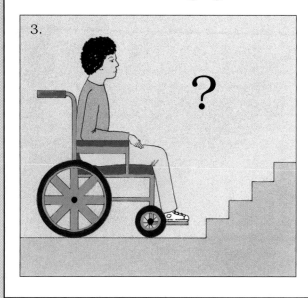

3. How could you make it possible for a person in a wheelchair to get up a short flight of stairs without being lifted by someone else?

New towns

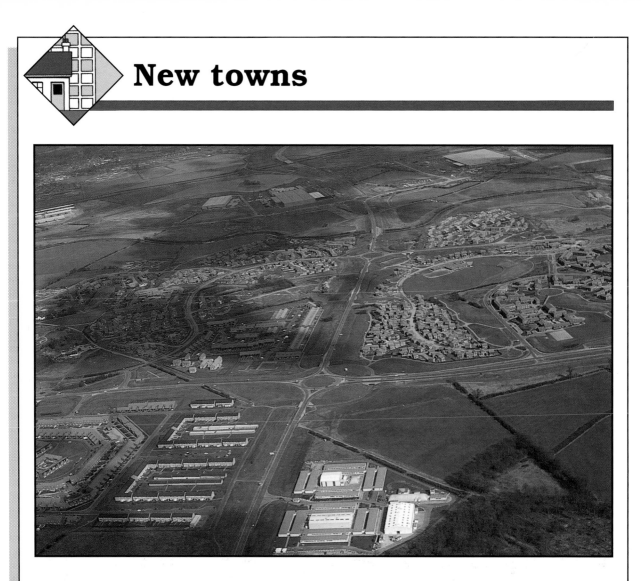

An aerial view of this new town shows how it was planned.

The opportunity to design a new town is rare but as the world's population grows, the need for new towns increases. One vital need of any town is that it should have a balanced cross-section of the population. Interests must be provided for the young and support given to the elderly. It is crucial that the community planners consider many important factors. These should include employment opportunities, transport, road and rail links, shopping centres with a balanced range of shops, health facilities such as doctors, medical centres and hospitals, water supplies, sewage and waste disposal.

Just as important is the consideration and siting of recreational centres like parks, playgrounds and swimming pools. Some of these may only work when the town reaches a certain size, but town planners have to think of future needs as a town grows and changes.

Draw a map

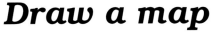

When visitors come to stay it is nice to have a map that shows helpful and interesting places near your home. Do not make it too big – a 10 km radius around your house should be enough for most people.

1. From a large-scale map of your area trace the main features around your house – roads, rivers, lakes, forests, railway lines, bus and train stations, the police station, hospital, library and historic buildings such as castles and churches.

You will need
A large-scale map of your area
A compass
Tracing paper
Local tourist information leaflets
Coloured pens

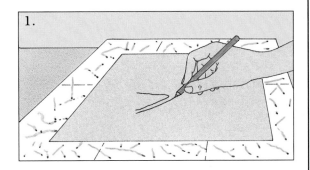

2. Do a little research about the important buildings in your area. For example, when were they built? Who was the architect?

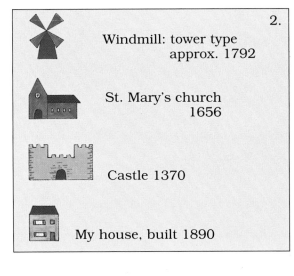

Windmill: tower type approx. 1792

St. Mary's church 1656

Castle 1370

My house, built 1890

3. Design a key of symbols to explain the features on your map. Use colour to make the symbols stand out.

4. If you are going on holiday you could research the area you will be visiting. Draw a map and make a list of interesting places for day-trips.

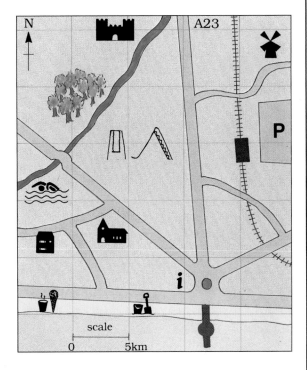

N   A23

P

i

scale
0   5km

Glossary

Aerated Blown full of air bubbles.

Appliance A tool which uses electricity to make it work.

Asphalt A natural black, sticky substance, similar to tar, used to waterproof roofs.

Cavity wall A wall built from two walls with a space between them, joined together with special links.

Cellar A room at the bottom of a house constructed below ground level.

Concrete A mixture of sand, cement and water used for floors and foundations.

Geothermal springs Water that has been heated deep below the Earth's surface.

Humidity A measure of the amount of water in the air.

Imported Brought in from a foreign country.

Infra-red A special kind of light which cannot be seen by the human eye.

Insulate 1. To prevent heat from getting out (if you want to keep warm) or getting in (if you want to keep cool). 2. To cover electrical components with a safe surface to prevent electric current from escaping.

Joist A length of wood or metal used to support floors, ceilings or other structures.

Lintel A long flat stone or piece of timber, as used over a door or window.

Mason A tradesperson skilled in the art of working with stone.

Mortar A mixture of sand, cement, lime and water used to fix bricks and stones together.

Population The number of people living in a named area.

Pre-fabricate To build at some place other than the final site and then transport to the site for assembly.

Roof truss A timber or metal framework that spans the walls of a building and supports the roof.

Scaffolding A temporary timber or metal framework put up to support workers during the erection or repair of a building.

Solar panel A device for collecting energy from the sun.

Thatch A thick waterproof layer of straw or reed used to make a roof.

Thermostat A temperature-sensitive device that controls heating or cooling systems.

Yurt A circular tent made of skin or felt used by Mongolian nomads.

 # Further information

Books to read

James, A. *Castles and Mansions* (Wayland, 1988)
Lambert, M. *Electricity* (Wayland, 1987)
Lambert, M. *Homes in the Future* (Wayland, 1988)
Langley, A. *Timber* (Wayland, 1986)
Rickard, G. *Building Materials* (Wayland, 1989)

Tools and equipment

All the projects can be made with simple hand tools.

Junior hacksaws are good for cutting wood. Blades need to be sharp and secure in the frame with the teeth pointing forwards.

Panel-pin hammers are the easiest for small hands to use.

A wheel-brace hand drill and a selection of drill bits (2 mm to 9 mm) will make essential holes.

Combination pliers are good for cutting, bending, twisting and holding.

Screws may be either slotted or crosshead, so a screwdriver to suit each sort is essential. Pick ones with comfortable handles that are not too large for the screws you will use.

Some form of work-holding device will make any project very much easier. Gee cramps, a small clamp-on table vice, or a work platform are good choices.

You may have to buy wood. Try to do this economically by setting out shapes on paper first, but remember that it is easier to make straight, rather than jigsaw-type cuts. Check also to see if the grain direction of the timber is important.

It might also be more efficient to stock up for two or three projects at once.

Join timber with screws, panel pins and woodworking glue. PVA glue is excellent, but it must be squeezed tight with pins, screws or cramps and left overnight to dry.

For a smooth finish, use glass-paper on wood.

Apply colour to wood with colouring felts, or acrylic 100 paints so that brushes can be washed in water. Use an exterior-quality paint for models that may be exposed to the weather.

All work should be carried out on a secure, steady surface. Protect the work surface with newspaper. Keep your tools in good order by storing them in a tool storage unit.

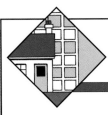

Places to visit

Australia

Master Builders Association
(In the capital city of your state.)

Museum of Applied
Arts and Sciences
500 Harris Street
Ultimo
N.S.W. 2007

See if you can arrange to visit your local do-it-yourself shop. Perhaps your parents could take you. Then you will be able to see all kinds of building materials from bricks and cement to windows and doors.

Britain

The Building Centre
26 Store Street
London WC1E 7BT

The Young Designers Centre
Design Centre
28 Haymarket
London SW1Y 4SU

Another good source of information is your local tourist office. Write to them, enclosing a stamped, addressed envelope, asking for details of houses, castles and churches in your area that might be worth visiting.

Notes for parents and teachers

Teachers will find this book useful in implementing the National Curriculum at levels 1, 2, 3 and 4 for Technology. *Houses and Homes* can be developed as a cross-curricular topic involving history, art and design.

There are many activities in this book that will require the help of a teacher or parent. Parents will also find the section on places to visit helpful during weekends and school holidays.

Index

Picture acknowledgements

The photographs in this book were supplied by: Bruce Coleman 4 (John Anthony), 8 (Roger Wilmshurst), 17 (Harald Lange), 42 (Eric Crighton); Eye Ubiquitous 6 (Nick Howarth), 11 (A. Carroll), 14 (Joe Pasieka), 16, 18 & 34 (Paul Seheult), 27 (S.K. Jold); Hutchison 25 (Chris Johnson); National Trust Photo Library/Ian Shaw 20; Tony Stone Worldwide *cover*; Topham 13, 32, 37; Wayland Picture Library 22, 24, 28, 30, 35; Zefa 10 (Nick Holt). All the illustrations were supplied by Jenny Hughes.